Trio Gets Stuck

Written by Lisa Thompson
Paintings by Ritva Voutila

Trio was running. He didn't look where he was going. He ran headfirst into the big tree. The tree house shook.

"Are you all right?" asked River.

"No, my horn is stuck in the tree," said Trio.

River and Pebble tried to pull Trio free.

No luck. Trio stayed stuck.

"We need help," said Pebble.

River went to find help.

River found Speck. Speck tried to pull Trio free. They all pulled.

No luck. Trio was still stuck.

Tickles was flying over the jungle.

"Need some help?" she asked.

"Yes please," said River.

Tickles tried to pull Trio free. They all pulled.

No luck. Trio was still stuck.

River asked Club to help.

Club tried to pull Trio free. They all pulled.

No luck. Trio was still stuck.

"I am going to be stuck forever," said Trio.

"I'll get more help," said River.

River asked Brock to help.

Brock tried to pull Trio free. They all pulled.

No luck. Trio was still stuck.

River had an idea. He told everyone to hide.

Suddenly, the jungle shook. Rex roared and stomped. He was hungry.

"Help! Help!" yelled Trio. He jumped and twisted.

Rex came closer. Rex roared and snapped his jaws. He was very hungry.

Trio wriggled and squirmed.

Suddenly, Trio's horn came unstuck. Trio was free! He ran away fast. He made sure to look where he was going. He was too afraid to look back.

"Well done, River," said Pebble. "You sounded just like the real Rex."

"It is the real Rex," said River. "Quick — run!"